THE

SPEA

To Harry
all the very best —

The Hill Speaks
ELSA CORBLUTH

Also by Elsa Corbluth

POETRY COLLECTIONS
St Patrick's Night (Peterloo Poets, 1988)
The Planet Iceland (Peterloo Poets, 2002)

POETRY BOOKLETS
Stone Country (Outposts)
Brown Harvest (Word and Action)
I looked for You (Crewe+Alsager College of Higher Education)

First Published in 2008
by Jurassic Press
Hawthorn Cottage, Rodden,
Near Weymouth, Dorset DT3 4JE

**A catalogue record for this book is available
from the British Library**

ISBN 980-0-9558870-0-0

Printed by Creeds, Broadoak, Bridport, Dorset DT6 5NL

ACKNOWLEDGEMENTS

Acknowledgements are due to the editors of the following anthologies and journals in which some of these poems first appeared:

Arts Council of Great Britain Anthologies 3 and 6, PEN Anthology, Bridport Arts Competition Anthologies, Proof 2 (South West Arts), Poets' England, Dorset, Anthology, Lancaster Festival Anthology, Dorset Year Book, "Poems on Hardy" (Word and Action) Outposts, Orbis, Samphire, The Rialto, Poetry Digest, Meridian, Poetry on the Lake Anthology, Pick, South.

Beach Sculpture, (Eype, Dorset) won 1st prize in the Poetry on the Lake Competition, formal category.

Skagen won 1st prize in the Orbis Rhyme International Competition, open class.

Jew won 1st prize in an early Bridport Arts competition.

Elin and *Hammer*, won supplementary prizes in later Bridport Arts competitions.

Corpse Road, Mardale, Cumbria won 2nd prize in the Dillington Competition.

Alpine was read on Poetry Now (BBC Radio 3)

For Adam, who helped me with the Icelandic.

CONTENTS

DORSET AND THE SOUTH

ICELAND AND THE NORTH

ELSEWHERE

DORSET
AND THE SOUTH

THE HILL SPEAKS

I am down on the Ordnance Survey map
As Merry Hill. The insignificant hamlet
at my foot takes its name from me.
I am also known as Eternal,
one of the Dorsetshire Eternals, you could say.
Only joking. I hear them all speak,
owners of little feet that go over me,
or round or beside me, or which
accelerate their vehicles, not even slowing down
to take a glance at me. I hear them all.
They could hear me if they bothered to listen.
Yes, I do have my little jokes,
ruts in my sides, deep mud where the gates are,
burdock. But my best joke is letting
the sun come down to me, very, very slowly,
then suddenly, grabbing it, dropping it
into my top pocket, and pretending it doesn't
exist. When the moon comes around
to my side of the lane, I have wonderful
games with it; these are more secret and special,
and for those eyes awake beyond their bedtimes
or in the winter lane without their cars.

New moon's a piece of white-gold wedding ring
and a round harvest moon's a Cox's apple
left to ripen and come down in its own time.

I have been told I am not large
as hills go: I can see the ridge
up there beyond me. I have heard them say
that, also, is not high, comparatively.
I have had them point at me and say
"What a dear little hill!" I have overheard:

11

"I am not good, normally, at climbing hills,
but I could manage that."

I am a way to and from. I am also
a thing in myself. They forget that,
tramping across me, sowing and reaping me,
picking primroses, blackberrying, hurrying over me
to get to the sea, or merely using me
as a viewpoint, the long white arm of the backwater
flung out towards the Isle of Slingers,
close as your hand when it's about to rain
or far away in haze. I've seen it all.

The traffic passing by me only comes
to avoid the main road. It very seldom stops here.

I have my share of rabbits, more than my share
of birds, (rooks, close-knit as a black shawl
until it tears and scatters
or a white cloud of gulls in from the sea),
cows, sheep, humanity in all its phases,
though this is sparse. And, as I hear them saying,
on winter evenings you can "hear the silence".

That's Merry Hill minding its own business.

A LITTLE LIGHT RAIN
(Puddletown Forest, Dorset, near Thomas Hardy's birthplace)

A little light rain kept you in your car.
The pointed woods were mine for playing in.
Rain was not felt as wet but smelt, a scent-bringer,
the stacked logs resinous.

I walked afloat,
the rhododendron faces
like waterlilies open on the rain.
Under bark and fungus
spells were being stirred.

Even in Dorset woods
some small domestic trolls may still be found
waking with sap
to jump on last year's cones
in vivid new-sprung bracken
snap twig fingers.

I take one by the hand back to your car
and wonder, could it live
in the green anarchy of our back garden
between the unpruned ornamental shrubs
and the prone elm tops?

I shall not want to come here now with you
when sunlight ribbons through like maypole braids
and brings out all the people from their cars.

This is a dark green place for loneliness
and Nordic fantasies
which was, one time, a dark green book to house
the pulled-back tortoise head
of that now fêted, garlanded, engraved
native of green ways and of difficult loves.

CLIFF COUPLE

Her hair was white as foam
On her man's arm.

(Forked shadows of the gulls,
Thrift pink as shells.)

Her head was white as cloud
In his chest's shade.

We usually see the young
Sculpted two into one;

Stories are told, songs sung
Centred upon the young

Whose elders stay at home
And to no dark towers come.

Only the golden go to Samarkand
And stand on moonlit boat decks hand in hand.

Could mother never stride
The shining green cliff side

Flying her white
Hair like a kite?

GREEN

Drowning in green after the raining petals,
the cherry holds green sprays of hard fruit nodules
among long dripping leaves. The toy green apples
are brushed with crimson and rain-sharpened grasses
have shot out of control.

Only the many-coloured spires of lupins,
the honeysuckle blanket, comfrey's purple,
heavy with bees, rival the green excesses.

Last evening a rainbow threw a long
bright-coloured silk scarf over the whole scene.
Willows lightened to lime in the sun's floodlight
that browned the may to golden, with a backdrop
sky as dark as drenched quarried stone.

April was August, cracking the baked clay
underfoot. Now, feet squelch into
soft mud throughout May, legs wade the knee-deep grass
and daylong April play of cloud and light
flows to the brink of June. Before my year's
first sea-swim, on a full moon's night awake,
I hear high waves rear at the shingle bank
a gull-flight's mile away. I hear them roll
and growl. I breathe with them.

                        Tomorrow morning
those green grass curves will build and crash, unheard
through village noises, work and birds and voices,
and the grass tide will rise as the skies open.

COME JUNE

Throw back your griefs like dogfish from the net
all my hurt darlings
and haul the good year in.

Heap up the hurts like weeds upon a bank
all my dear dreamers
and burn them to the ground.

Gather your dreams like roses for the house
all my far travellers
and breathe them as you pass.

Swallow your travels like a slap-up meal
my precious tired ones
and sleep the good night out.

This year begins when stones are warm enough
all my brave swimmers
and will not finish yet.

DAFFODILS OF WAR (March 2003)

They line the lanes. They riot in the gardens.
The sun's a daffodil, its points of yellow
piercing the branches. Nights, the wakeful moon
stares into windows light of a white daffodil.

Our season opens. Colour returns. But a curtain,
thick as a sandstorm, descends and drab as a desert,
to picture the attacks and the nights of burning.

The world is maturing, and yet it is governed by children.
Real children are filling the streets, saying NO. They are older
than those grown in years who make their nations' decisions.

Daily the "friends" are killing and wounding their allies,
the quick-fire cowboys shooting whatever lives.

My teenaged daughter died from "friendly fire".
An alcoholic in the house of refuge
the girl had come that night to help, had lighted
the blaze that killed ten people. Her crazed motive
was to be praised for putting out the flames.
But, like all fires, it did not know its boundaries,
and like all wars, it had no definable limits.

Twenty years ago in a grey town centre
I chanced upon a straggling demonstration
of women dressed in black with daffodils
held in their hands, of babies in prams, the flowers
spiking yellow stars upon their covers,
silently trumpeting their pleading message,
to ban this country's mass destruction weapons.

They mimed earth's funeral. I joined the quiet procession
of black-clothed mourners, daffodils like candles
against grey stone in the grey afternoon,

through grey English streets to the Town Hall entrance
and there one sang in a pure voice, a warning,
and on the steps we left our daffodils.

I thought of the eighteen daffodils we cradled
for our daughter's funeral, one for each of her years.
On each March since I have placed the eighteen flowers,
gleaming, upon her grave. But this year's daffodils
stand there for all the dead and the young dead
of needless war, whatever their allegiance,
and the dead children and the broken of the fire-"freed" cities

while daffodils blow gently through this unspoiled village,

NOBODY'S

She is nobody's
grandmother.
Nobody
peeps back at her
out of the vermillion
constellations
of rose hips,
nobody giggles
into the crimson
hawthorn, juggles
with waxy snowberries,
pink spindle knuckles.

Nobody glistens
with pin-head rain
under fairylights of bryony,
gives her from inky hands
rain-bloated blackberries,
learns not to touch nightshade,
how to tell
mushrooms from deathcaps.

Nobody
wears fancy crabapples
over the ears
like cherries,
calls, look at me, look at me,
bites on the bitter sloes
before frost
sweetens them.

Nobody, nobody
blows down the last of the leaves
like candle flames
from a birthday cake.

LUPINS

They are on the rampage, gorgeous
warriors in full plumage,
each fat plume war-dancing in warm wind,
purples, yellows, pinks, white, with their leaves' green petals.

If I zoom in to the floret details
each is an open pincer like a crab's,
but puffed, a small two-branched balloon,
one part shell pink, the other burgundy
or cream with lemon, mauve with white. Bees enter.
My lens allows my eye to probe that entrance
while my nose is tickled by their peppery breath.

Pull back again: each bloom is a tower, pointed,
and part way up from base it changes colour:
pinks into yellows, purples into whites
and many variations. From my door I cannot see beyond them
to spaces without lupins. They have taken over.

Skyscraper flowers, sprung up behind my back
quite unintended. I had planned a bed
of colour close to earth, petunias, mimulas, pansies,
faces that looked up appealingly, knowing their place,
and allowed an elegant view of lawns and fruit trees.
I never invited this overbearing brilliance.

I remember travelling in New Zealand.
At Mount Cook lupins marched across the valley,
surged, exploding rainbows, filling summer stream beds,
rioting round the feet of stern white mountains.
Miles of lupins. When I stopped to praise them
a ranger explained, "We don't want them. We're trying to spray
them away. This is National Park you see. They're not natives."

And I'm confused. It wasn't as through the area
was full of Maoris. I recalled our plane being sprayed
inside, with us still in it, entering Wellington airport,
and the two-hour queue for agricultural inspection
to make sure that we weren't carrying foreign fruit.

So, who were the invaders? You'd have thought that the pink faces,
or sun-dyed brown, and tall legs would have felt themselves
kin to the lupins.

                    When the Soviet authorities decided
to plant lupins at Chernobyl because lupins
absorb radioactivity they grew them
to be ploughed in very deeply, glorious martyrs.

IMPRINTING

That duckling thinks he's her mother.
That old drake
has left mate, nest, native
speckle-downed eel grass,
sky-chip damselflies,
bulrush busbies, bridal swans,
sun-netted brackish lake,
because she's on his tail,
her little wet webbed tracks
trailing him into that role.

Maternally, he takes her
under his wing. She hears
his collusive quacking.
This stills her flapping.
She is impressed. Her impression
impresses him. He is thinking
he must have given birth
to the egg her little beak
came through, to see him looking.

For that, he's flown his home
ground, home water,
cracked his own brood
apart, as a boy's stone
shoots a pond's ice,
makes a black star.
It is what they believe they are
that carries them on to the flood
and into the length of a cloudy unswum river.

FUN WORLD (April 1986. Weymouth. Bombing of Libya,
Queens 60th Birthday.)

Men are demolishing the unsafe pier.
It has two small towers striped in primary colours
like sugar sticks of Victorian childhoods
and, beneath these, a building curved like a lighthouse
which held the bandstand. It has pictures of balloons,
a bunch, red, green, yellow in a royal blue concrete sky.
Above the balloons there is scarlet painted lettering:
"FUN WORLD". They have set light to the main structure.
flames spurt. The pier is a ship stranded
in heavy fog and alight. Smoke blows along the beach.
The blue spring day is furred, blurred to a white-out, chilled.

A mile away, along the steaming sand,
at the cloud-swallowed harbour I have realised
the coincidence of sea mist meeting the smoke
and unrelated. But my eyes have already established
the link, and will not break it. Nor will my other senses.

Fog quietens the sea front, sharpens cries of children.
Fog listens to the thunder of aimed weights
swung against FUN WORLD – now a matchstick model –
like a series of explosions.

Even ten miles
farther west in my home inland hamlet
there is mist paling the queenly daffodils
and moistening blue hyacinths to the scent of bereavement
outside comprehension.

Fun World ablaze. Blasted.
Cloud filling world. World become cloud. World cold.

23

HOW TO MAKE A LEGEND

Adam stood in the garden
looking at snakes
under the apple trees.

He let the adder
draw its two black
ric-rac lines
smooth, off the edge of his thoughts.

One or two golden slowworms
played snakes around his feet.

Adam is now eleven.
In May our Eden
is full of brilliant
pointed grass
painted by Henri Rousseau
our sky is lit
with flowering apple.
Under, the snakes come, warming.

Reptiles, eyes of the sea,
stones of the sky,
Adam collects.
People, and what they say, are less arresting:
spiking grass clumps
stringing out of clouds,
onslaught of waves
his animation.

                         Cold gut of a sea cave
                         I share with him
                         to different ends.

He knows he could more easily
lose his way among

the undersides of words
than lose a snake's
route in the grass,
a limpet's logic
washing back to
its home rock.
All the sky's mathematics
can fit in his pockets.

I do not know him well.
He was born sleeping,
tired from his long
journey to man,
the slow blind heading for light.

He is the longest poem
we are making
we cannot stay
long enough to finish it.

PLANET PORTLAND

Iceland was less strange
                in its cinder deserts,
Lapland in drizzling twilight
                was less desolate
than this suburban moonland,

this worn old tooth
                attached by one thin strand
to the reassuring
                English face of Weymouth.
Sundays have scuffed its Pulpit.
                Shack of cafes.
steam "Teas" and swell with doughcakes.

Bony in flowering South,
                its main crop stone,
no proper island
                but an overnight
St. Kilda at some tides,
                that land's-arm keeps
a freak sea up its sleeve,

harbours spare gales,
                when the whole boat is pushed,
an old tug to unaccustomed
                to deep oceans,
on the high wave's contours.

All burrows, moon-holed,
                    carious with caverns.
Grained in its part-time islanders
                    this superstition:
never, whatever you do,
                    mention those puff-tailed
hopping mammals
                    just in case you end up,
your frayed rope
                    to the mainland severed,
put out to sea for ever.

THE SIZE OF STONEHENGE

"It's smaller than I thought." Of course. It would be
at this permitted distance, (even if we allow
for childhood places to shrink on later visits)
the Stones diminished by the souvenir shop –
pre-Christian power depicted on a teatowel –
the lavatorial subway, close barbed wire
fencing them from us, models in a theme park,
the queue to view, the roaring road we dare
to shoot across, to avoid payment, getting
as near for a photograph as with a ticket.

Fifty years back, in my gingham frock
or an aunt's cut-down coat, according to season,
I walked the twenty miles from Salisbury and back,
ducked underneath the wire (I hadn't the pennies
for the little turnstile.) No-one seemed to notice.
I was often alone with the Stones. They were huge then.
They would give me shade from the Plains' open sunlight
or they and I would be hidden in the mist.

I knew their shapes but not their names, except
that one was the Altar Stone. At summer solstice
the sun was sacrificed, bled on the giant table,
rarely, when clouds were absent. Then the pagan
miracle appeared. I never saw it.
Teenaged, I cycled with a friend. No moon.
Stones high in watery dawn. Two or three cars
nearby, a handful of people.

                         In the sixties
we took our children. There were few besides
ourselves. The children hid and screamed and chased
each other in between the towering Stones.

Then came the Hairies. Our teenagers among them.
They swayed and sang and sweated, strummed and drummed,
chewed up the ground with toothless tyres, swallowed
pills that lit up their heads like a full moon
when no sun rose. And those Stones were gargantuan.
The battles followed. Police. Glass and Mud. Convictions.
New laws. New fence. In place of wheel tracks, litter,
more lasting, concrete, landmarks. And, removed,
like mountains viewed through a wide-angle lens
to get more in, the Stones' belittling.

POCKETS (Dartmoor)

"Pockets" she said, one who guarded her acres
of old rock and new fencing
in a niche of moorland,
protected favourite trees with little cages,
kept a pack of diminutive
yapping bitches
and kept a mumbling man
making her walls,
sorting the bolts and hinges,
and who kept three
aristocratic horses,
six swan-white geese
and fifteen golden hens:
"When the bomb comes there will be pockets
where a few of us will live quite unaffected.
Everyone won't be annihilated."

"And if they are?"
"In that case, man
is so vile
he deserves it."

"And the geese and hens?"
And the sleek horses?
And the dainty dogs?
And the beloved

                        trees?

TRANSPORT (Sark)

No cars allowed on the island:
for the rest of your day
or the rest of your life
if your mind was made up
like the climb of the tide
to the fit of its stain on the land
you could learn to be driven
by one foot in front of the other
and one thought in front of the other,
and every breath breathed
would go right through your head
and you would be only
transported by joy
or the grief of its having to end
when the waves that you ride
would bellow and crack
in the hollowed out head
of the land that your head
cannot keep.

SAVE THIS AUTUMN (Sark)

When the wind began to beat
the heat out of the evening
and to beat peaks of white
on to the dark blue water,
when the next day's end spread mist
up to the garden's hedge,
I said, hold the summer, do not
lose it yet, my brown arms' sun-white hairs
standing defiant at the year's droop.

When the lighthouse turned its eye
full stare on our homecoming
and hydrangea pinks and blues
had faded to pale coffee,
when the blocks of cliffs were stacked
neatly behind the boat-tails,
I said, keep the island, do not
pack it away like a toy
for other people's children.

When the people came inside
to curtain off the sky-change
and the yellow roomlight cancelled
the outer yellow stonelight,
when the air was tidied up
to a rattle in the windows,
I said, save this autumn, do not
trade it in for the frost
of a less forgiving winter.

OLD WIVES' TALE

After a certain date in October in Dorset
the devil pees on the blackberries.
He's done it this year all right,
after containing himself all summer
pissing down all night,
all week, the whole of October.

Through the burnt quarter
of the year we were guiltily browning,
as the hills tanned, hardened,
smoked and blackened,
thinking drought the devil's,
dreading a dry autumn,

but now Old Nick is out in his gumboots
kicking tin cans through the heavens,
tipping his slops down streets
and over the floors of good people,
while greenlit fields
are goggling white with mushrooms,

and as for the blackberries?
Inky blobs for fingernails of witches,
wickedly wet,
bejewelled with deadly nightshade.
Come out, dry maidens:
before the winter gather devil's fruit!

SWIMMERS

I think of London's literary men
swimming in Hampstead Ponds
in black of winter,
stern bending trees like silent editors,
mist rising from the early morning water.

then think of my maternal grandfather
breaking ice on the Serpentine
to dive, while the ducks walked
on the park lake's cold skin.

He was not literary,
but literate, reader of "Titbits"
(before it was cut into squares
 for the outside lavatory.)
Married at seventeen,
he fathered eleven children,
earned two sovereigns weekly
by cycling to collect
his neighbours' "on tick" payments,

took his family to Purley, then "the country",
on the penny tram from Croydon,
for a days' holiday,
the three virgin eldest
to be servants to their parents'
old age, their father's deafness,
perhaps resulting from those shivery dives,
their mother gone at the knees
from all that weight of babies.

Then I think about my mother
in 1910, aged nine, stitching
old pillow ticking, to produce
that time's striped bathing costume,
the stiffness of the fabric
on her stick-like little person
spoiling her dreams of swimming.

Again I think of London's bearded authors
breaking a pond's smoothness, making a forked pattern
as ducks do, carving the surface, with the trees hunched over
reading the day's story on the page of water.

CHARTWELL

The man of blood let no red roses
bleed in among the gold.
The man of sweat kept a cool fish garden.
The man of toil built a wall of bricks
against Kent breezes.
The man of tears
painted propped birthday cards of woods,
fields amateur baize green
and gentlemen in period shorts
at summer tables.

Did he never say:
I would rather have painted that picture;
that Guernica, than have taken
some bits of Berlin, the hand of a queen,
another cigar box, a state laying out?

Indoors the queue is given
tasteful upholstered stingless memory-pats:
along with muted braided lady furniture
are glass-cased uniforms,
while outside, this unpromising cold Easter,
above the wedged cars
and the whitethroat daffodils
the British sky is khaki.

(The town of Westerham, Kent, near Chartwell, Churchill's
house, has a statue of General Wolfe, who said he "would
rather have written that poem" – Gray's "Elegy" – "than
have taken Quebec.)

LITTLE BROTHER SPIDER
(for a friend afraid of them)

If this velvet room were mine,
nights satin lined,
padded from baser London,
and if a small September morning
got in between the muslin
and brought a spider with it
which Tarzanned softly down the trembling curtain
and gave a soundless solitary chase
across the carpet, I would bow it in,
I would say, welcome dancer, enter, dance.

My home is where lush autumns
poke bulbous cartoon noses of mushrooms
through dripping morning grass
and where the midnight rains send in tall spiders.
On my stone floors I almost hear them rustle.

I was not always this quiet audience.
Time was when all those legs
could frighten and alarm,
those many darknesses,
that monstrous ballet,
menace of tickling speed.

Now, menace has new bodies
and needs no legs to travel.

Fear now the death of trees,
fear cancer sucking faces into brown
or your house driven down
and you set in a new tower
farther from spiders,
and fear dying air.

DAYFLOWER (Morning Glory, Heavenly Blue)

Daylight whisks them open,
strings of blue bunting
out of night's hat conjured.
Early, they are streaked with purple:
sun, topping the trees, turns them
into pure sky-blue glad-rags.

At noon, wide open,
with white starburst centres
and white wicks in their little flames of yellow,
theirs is that clear blue, unbelievable
as a June sky, cloud-free, perfect.

Evening deepens to royal,
gives back the stripes of violet.
Fragile Indian muslin darkens, droops,
shrivels to small pink scraps
to be picked off the next morning.

At night, in secret,
newly-lenghtened buds, slim cones like shells,
wait to unroll their spirals
into tomorrow's day-tricks.

Seeds of these magic flowers
were, for a time, unobtainable,
being hallucinogenic, so illegal –
but why hallucinate when this reality
is, in itself, "unreal, man"?

In this window
the daylong, dayshort drama
is enacted: surprise, laughter, pathos,
curtain up, climax, finale.

As the year winds down
autumn, like day's end, darkens and marks them,
bugles inaudible last posts through them.

Sometimes, October ending,
when light is charged with all the downward changes,
wide cobalt blues bloom side by side
with limp and sad pink-purples
as though uncertain of the time of day or season.

I wait to see how long the final few
hang, in the contracted winter days,
like room-dried butterflies.

WINTER HAIKUS

The longest night past
white days lengthen to open
the first cold snowdrops.

Red camellia
offers rosy hands towards
the still-distant spring.

Snow blossoms on black
branches: January blooms
tinsel at sunrise.

Children make snowmen
as though with white plasticine:
cold friends fill their dreams.

The thawing snowman
hunches into the landscape
as though he's homeless.

Frost in the furrows:
tweed woven on the field's loom:
the hill wears a skirt.

In deep Dorset lanes
wind fashions snow drifts into
wild sea waves and swans.

In Finnish forests
you ski, you stay on the road,
or else – snow's waist deep.

When Eskimos no
longer live in igloos, they
buy icecream from Danes.

Lapps drove their reindeer
where Chernobyl's cloud drifted.
Their future's less clear.

Reykjavik children
skate in the city centre,
lug sledges to school.

In Iceland's fjords,
dark for six weeks, the returned
sun starts a party.

TO A WIND FROM ALL DIRECTIONS IN A CHANGING CLIMATE (Terza rima / sonnet)

All seasons' wind, throughout the year returning,
Moving the trees in summer like sea waves,
Loud like a tide-rush on a winter morning.

In spring and autumn surging through the caves
Of arching boughs, you are the messenger
Of seasonal confusion, when new leaves

Are stripped, and when, ferociously, you tear
Full blossoms to the ground and sever limbs
From August beech trees, carelessly lay bare

A lush green forest with the power that dreams
Can hold, when solid objects melt or bend
And break established laws, so that it seems

A year-long equinox with no real end,
You almost ever-present, tidal, wind.

SONG AT THE DECEMBER SOLSTICE

In the loch of the world's tears
I can no longer swim
Losing the skills of years
In every limb.

On the hills of the world's pain
I can no longer climb
Having no power to gain
Extended time.

At the end of the shortest day
Seeps out the meagre light.
There is not any way
To hold back night.

The black sea hits the shore
And does not ever sleep.
The closed sky shows no star
And windows weep.

In the valley of all loss
The day crawls, pallid-faced,
And winter limps across
The plains of waste.

SPRING CLEANING

Where marriages
are made on paper

There are papers
on how to bring
up the children,

there are girls'
walls papered
with the throats of boys,
their eyes like swimming pools,

and in among the grit
and metal bits
in boys' pockets
are the furtive
cigarette papers,

and the shelves of men,
bent beneath treaties,
shoulder their share
of shiny paper nudes
coy in brown envelopes.

There a woman could
live all her story
like a park keeper's
spiked stick

if it wasn't that
outside all this
paper work

are half-inch heavens
of speedwell weeds,
a slice of sea their colour,
air to be sipped
with slow daring,

and underneath
all the waste paper

are rustling people's
wants and angers

and such treasures.

Feed them: they are all here for the last time.

PRIORITIES (Film: L'enfant Sauvage)

Tears have no uses for the forest boy.
They will not help him kill a fastening dog
or climb from running men,

so do not teach him sorrow.

Rivers are for his thirst.
He needs no hygiene in his coils and hollows
being in danger of no man-diseases.

Do not bath him like a pet.

No alphabet will teach him where nuts hide
or how to stalk his meat
or that the leaves heal wounds.

Bring him no books. Books eat a forest down.

Forget your house. Shed your professional shirt.
Live among trees. Wait. Perhaps paw the ground.
If he comes sniffing you

Together you may move two million years.

BEACH SCULPTURE (Eype, Dorset)
(For Rúnar, born in Iceland)

I made a baby out of grey cliff clay,
Fashioned his starfish hands, his round fish mouth,
Moulded his man-parts in the soft sea spray,
Grandmothered son of Adam in the south.
My mind-born baby soon the next high tide
Would take. His risen belly, baby feet,
The creeping foam would crumble and the wide
Ocean would swallow. When the summer heat
Had dried his rock base, then the empty stone
Would show no trace. His living counterpart
Would thrive to swim warm pools when he had grown
Strong in a colder land. My unskilled art

That bore a legendary child of mud
Willed glad survival for the child of blood.

SLEEPING BEAUTY or
The Ballad of Kilburn
(In memory of the girl helper who died at the Mother Teresa hostel)

The witch was only six years old.
They took no notice of a child

Who said, at Beauty's christening:
"Those gifts the other fairies bring

Will make you clever, rich and lovely,
Healthy, generous and lively.

Your bouncing babyhood will bloom,
Your childhood show no cloud of doom,

But, just as you have come of age
With all your gifts a gleaming page ..."

Cackling, the hag-child left. The Queen
And King and court ignored the scene.

The Princess grew with golden hair
And magic smile for all to share,

But when her eighteenth birthday came
She fancied God had called her name.

The witch had now become a nun
Who said: "Come in, my pretty one,

Our Lord will need young girls to work
For him:" she gave a holy smirk:

"There is a house where you may do
The good your Saviour wants you to."

This building sheltered homeless people,
Some of whom were known to tipple,

One of whom lit fires in churches –
Just the place for one who searches,

Starry-eyed with bright moon face,
To help the ones who fell from grace.

Oh witches can be good, we know,
And so can water, so can snow

And so can fire, to bake a cake,
But not for drunken hands to take

And make a blaze to light the dark
Like fireworks in a city park

So that ten. sheltering from frost,
Homed in the walls of flame, were lost.

Witches in white, haloed with blue,
Had been too eager good to do

One smoke-detector to install.
The plaster Virgin on the wall

Survived, but, laid among the dead,
The once-gold girl with faceless head.

GODSONG

God of the bloodlit sky,
the dark rooks circling,
god of the raw backwater,

god of the sodden Hill
the moist fields sweating silage,

god of the wind-walked house
and a clock's footsteps,
the cold lane of alone;

god of the guns of wind,
the sea's assault,
barrage of stony beach;

god of the risen gale,
late-budding roses
blackening with cold,

are you the same
god of the burning people,
god in the cupboard?

giver of soup and of psalms,
shrouder of women
in ashen habits?

Are you that one
dripping the light
out of the Dorset hills,

bringing back morning
after the burning?

ALPINE

Between the seasons of snow and summer,
the skis upended and paths unopened,
it is a time for daring and for caution,
the hanging pastures holding secret gentians,
snow running into crocuses and meadows
rainbowed with oxlips, campions and pansies,
the soft blue fringes of the soldanella;
the pinewoods hiding orchids.

He sent her up alone, said, in Swiss German,
"Above the chairlift platform there is danger
of avalanches: please walk DOWN the footpath."
She climbed to where the ridge turned into cornice,
the white wave of her three-day fascination,
and found a compromise between the seasons,
a space between the reckless and protection,
before she reached the forest.

where pines were melting in the greenest rain.

THE SMALL SCOTTISH PRIMROSE

The botanist said: "There's a small Scottish primrose
with nowhere to go but the sea and extinction
when the warming of weather creates oceans' rising."

When I bloomed on this beach with the blush of the sea-pinks,
vivid blue viper's bugloss and yellow horned poppy,
tanned brown as these cliffs built of sea-facing sandstone,

and swam in the waves I now hear in the distance,
then dreaming and waking were one. Now my dreaming
has little to do with the pain of my waking

but takes me on journeys and climbing and swimming.
My life's among leaves still. I wake to their surging
in light of my window, at storm tide of summer.

Alive, I have joy in the greening of gardens
and opening petals and blooming of daylight –
but if I am taken away from these spaces

the ocean of other will swallow me wholly
and shrink and engulf me and I will be nothing,
adrift from the land like the small Scottish primrose.

ICELAND
AND THE NORTH

ELÍN

"Litla, litla ..."
and the young man
in the Reykjavík
restaurant told that
not only Latins
crooning "Bambina!"
can be touched to
back-shivering awe
by such new hands
opening
unbelievable
flowers in a warm
room, but also
ice-lake-eyed
serious Nordic citizens
stepping in from the early
afternoon twilight
of Laugavegur,
catching sight of that
two-week old
fine-downed head top,
find in themselves warm springs
like those which heat
this winter town.

Bereaved of my girl child, I shared
this daughter, her girl mother,
hair gilded by the candle,
giving her girl her breast,
curtained by shadows.

On the summit of Esja
on the shortest day of the year
in a Viking sword of a wind
that slashed the snow to clouds
with the blond head of the sun
leaning on the horizon
in the slit of daylight
between dark and dark,
I celebrated
my first grandchild's
first month's birthday.

ICELANDIC MYTH (The origin of Icelandic Elf-folk)

Eve
must have lived in Iceland,
that paradise
of hot springs, northern lights,
red jasper in the mountain clefts,
white summer nights,
cheap thermal heat
in dark-day winters,
snow-caps like dishes
of gleaming skyr upturned,
rainbows and waterfalls,
and, of course, "Eden"
the tourist greenhouse museum at Hveragerði
(though that came later.)

She had a child each year.
No-one then had invented
any way not to.

Except:

God said "Apples
are out of bounds".
Eve took no notice.
Adam was just as bad
(if not worse.)

In Iceland, apple trees
(like "Eden's" bananas)
are grown in greenhouses
(so it was warm in there.)

Neither of them knew
that apples
were aphrodisiac.

Well, one day, ten years later,
God sent Eve
a message, writ in steam,
saying, "Have your children ready:
I'm coming down
to inspect them."

Eve panicked.
It was bath night,
and half her children
were in the tub.

She'd never have time
to wash the rest –
so she hid them
(thinking God wouldn't know
how many she had.)

The unwashed ones
became the Hidden People,
doomed to live forever
invisible to humans
(except to very few)
hiding in the hollows
of their lava homes.

Even the road makers
don't disturb them,
shaping roads around
the piles of lava
peopled by the dirty hidden ones.

On the whole they're friendly
if left alone,
but they've gone on reproducing
and there are now so many
that you never know
if they could take over.
In fact, they may even be secreting
Iraq's weapons
of mass destruction.

You wouldn't think of looking there,
would you?
Iceland
hasn't had a war
since the Vikings.

Those weapons,
like the elves,
need to be believed in
to govern action.

SKÓGAR SAGA

Steinn,
Einar,
running;

2am and a pink-faced moon,

black lava-dust beach,
toe-prints to moss-grey waves,
twilight becoming dawn;

smack of two men's feet along sea's edge.

Pause:
Einar
stoops,

scoops out
small shallow bowl in black sand,
takes from his pocket matches and

lights
incense:
sacred-pagan smell.

We all stand round it.

(Summer-cold, three hours east of Reykjavík.)

And no questions.

> In AD one thousand the Chief of the Althing
> At Thingvellir, lava-cleft parliament, had problems,
> the frequent wars with the Christian countries.
> He slept on it, waking next morning, decreed:
> "All Icelanders will now, by law, be Christian."

Ah, but church spires in these outlying places
are outlines merely, concrete drawings on air,
clouds or stars seen through them,
terns hoop-jumping their holy triangles,
sailing between their mythical Viking horns.

Steinn carves
foot-long letters in soot-sand –
runic symbols –
translates to Icelandic:
"góðviðri spáð á morgun," then for us,
"Fine day tomorrow"

It is tomorrow:
four hours' sleep and up again.

Skógafoss, Skógafoss,
let down your fine white hair,
giant rock-browed
troll-goddess,
and we will step up to the white
frozen pate
of your father,
Eyjafallajökull.

But we're starting late:
Einar and Steinn
first had to visit
the grave of Steinn's grandmother
at the foot of a gully,
under an ice claw,
watched over by tall northern elves
which could be mistaken
for rocks in their mosses and lichens.

Steinn is weighed down
with six bottles of non-alcoholic Malt.
He takes the whole lot in his shopping basket,
politely sweating in his green city mackintosh
(back at the Bank on Monday.)

Take, with a pinch of salt,
baby-faced Einar;
sells perfumes in Reykjavík market,
with his computer works out horoscopes
he embroiders, rose-bud innocent,
by means of what he's been told about clients.

Track higher, higher;
stars of pink stonecrop –
oh that blue!
the beyond-white snowcap
getting no
nearer.
In spite of no coming night
it is our return time.

Turn,
Stein.
Einar:
"We'll climb this mountain next year."
If so, doubtful with you, smooth-talking Einar.

Meantime, at Hotel Edda,
sun-scorched Steinn sleeps on a sofa,
tea on the table and the ubiquitous
unleavened sponge-cake striped with red glue-jam,
Prince Polo biscuits,
on such an afternoon, nectar and manna.

Evening wind rises,
tosses
Skógafoss's
long white mane
swinging with elves
as absolutely real
as Einar's promises.

Foss = waterfall

BJÖRK-SPEAK

Did you ever hear
Cockney with a sweet Icelandic accent? –
Björk at the South Bank.

Whereas many Icelanders
imbibe their English
from American movies,
she sipped hers in London –

so – it's not "liddle" but
"li'-le", while her lyrics are
not exactly sung, but
melodiously chanted,
from the time before hers
when the occupying Danes
banned music
and her people
devised their ringing stories
to be shouted
in long vowels
over the winds.

Her voice,
not drowned
by mix of instruments,
surmounting them like weather,
is laced with laughter.

Minute figure
in a large expanse,
she is used to
wide
spaces,
whether giant cliffs,
glacial waves
or enormous stages.
Wild, in psychedelic
lime green,
shocking pink
or any vivid
shade of paint
that livens her home town,
she runs on,
dominates
the huge performance space,
excited child.

When the builders of the new
Reykjavík
abandoned their turf homesteads,
put up their concrete
and corrugated iron,
painted metal roofs
a rainbow range of colours,
the elf folk took their children
out of the city
to hide in lava piles
and folds of rivers,
abseil down the ribbons
of waterfalls,

but one stayed,
turned change to her advantage
like an urban fox,
moved to a denser,
older, greyer city,
adopted its jokey
sophistication and an east end accent,
shed browns and pales
of stunted birch bark,
damp sheep, stubby ponies,
and dressed in brilliant
rippling viscose,

lithe as a thieving mink,
sprang on to car roofs,
throwing modulated screams
down amazed roads.

But, suddenly surprised
by curious recognition
crowding and closing
even into her space of private travel,
her Viking hackles rose,
the troll-wench, cornered,
clobbered a photographer.

No lofty Viking
with hair pale willow-fluff,
but straight-dark-maned,
slight slant of eyes,
(a touch of Inuit?)
that little nose upturned
like baby doll's
and the humorous mouth,

she sculpts her hair
into the wild designs
that fire the lava columns in her land.

Who else would dare
to ill-use with such charm
a borrowed language? –
to enunciate
"lumin*i*ous"
three times in one song,
and likewise to declare
" State of emergency –
how beautiful to be" –
(beautiful emergency?)

How about
a Björk dictionary?

Elusive?
some one caught her.
This child has a ten-years child.
She guards him from the gaze
of her own captured public.
Its child, she keeps limelight,
lime-green-light.
Chuckling, she tortures,
exquisitely
its language.

THE SCREAM BURGLARS

What will they do with stolen agony?
Where will they hide the skull-head, the mouth's O,
the hands denying ears sound of the visible
horror that tears the sky like raw meat, the late day's
shrill mad swirl of the fjord, the two friends
uninvolved, two small boats unaware?

How to sell torment and terror, the sight drenched
red with a bled dead sister, the fence empty
of farewell lovers, the face blenched
to bonelight, that foetal head
cradled in buried mother? Who dare price
panic in sky and sea and a death's head?

At the National Gallery, London,
after Munch's "Frieze of Life", saturated
with dread and death and dying, fever and fear,
loss and love's desperation, a humourless
northern landscape, climate of sharp daylight
and bitter darkness, the couple in front of me
at the bookstall shuddered visibly. She said to him "No,
I can't take any more. Let's go
somewhere where we can laugh." Over my coffee
I felt an absent picture's warmth creep back.

I remembered Oslo. Only an hour left
before the Munch Museum closed, after battling
with maps and tube trains without Norwegian.
One hour for Munch. The writhing, clinging, staring,
despairing, bleeding, screaming. Hasty tourist,
I hurried through the anguished images.

Minutes left, I ran back to his "Sun"
exploding into stabs of coloured light
from its white centre on to the blue inlet,
tinting the shore's smooth rocks and all the smiling
basalt islands, and the live yelling
burst of the day's head exorcised that "Scream"
so I took aim and shot – to steal – a photograph.

(Theft of Edvard Munch's painting "The Scream"
in 1994 and 2004 from the Munch Museum, Oslo.)

SIX IBSEN POEMS

EYOLF

All that clear
northern water,
the fjord, clear as eyes,
the eyes of Eyolf,
born eyes, drowned eyes,
eyes wide open,
hardly liquid
glacial water,
crevasse-green with
the crutch floating.

Deep dream water;
on the mind's bed
two white pebbles,
eyes of Eyolf.
Blind, the swimming
fisher children
cast their rags and
splash and chuckle.
All the hovels
of the harbour
lean to shield
the eyes of Eyolf.
Masts are bristling
like his lashes,
harbour spars are
wooden crutches,
shoals his fingers.

All that long
northern winter,
sky upended
flat black fjord,
stars the open
eyes of Eyolf,
Eyolf's parents
close their staring
house with shutters,
dream of harbouring
poor children
climbing with their
gull-like voices
up the fellside
for the firelight,
food and toys and
books of learning.

Still the huge
white eyes of Eyolf
like full moons at
home in darkness
penetrate
the secret corners:
mother, father,
and the fjord
like a dead black
wing between them.
All the children,
all the singing,
all the long
days of the summer,
yellow globe-flowers,

arctic gentians,
cannot close the eyes of
Eyolf.

(In Ibsen's play, LITTLE EYOLF, Eyolf, a crippled child,
drowns in the fjord while his parents are quarrelling.)

SOLVEIG

Peer was the one I married. He was not my son.
Forgive an aged woman her confusion.

It was because of his son, twisted in wits, half a troll,
gangling along at his back, that he had to leave us all,

old mother, wide-eyed girl, a troll's kingdom,
his limping, crooked heir, our forest home.

He built it, put me in, said, "Wait for my return,
my pure princess, my virgin: Peer Gynt is on the run.

His boy found his own hole inside some mountain.
Peer's troll-mate, never real, would not be seen again.

Peer, for whom I had lost myself in the dense wood,
went seeking his own self down all the world's roads,

seas, deserts, continents, met con-men, lunatics,
lechers – all self-seekers – and learned to play their tricks.

"Life" said Peer, meant "going dry-shod down time's stream."
Solveig, among the pines, sang only of him.

Like all the famous, Peer feared he'd be forgotten –
white-haired, crept back to her old-maiden's cottage,

cried, "Mother, help your son!" (She was long dead.)
Gullible, Solveig half-believed what he said.

Don't let me disappear into obscurity –
tell them all how BAD I've been so that they remember me."

Son, husband, little Peer, your crimes they are petty.
You traded idols? So, which kind? Here's the nitty-gritty:

Mala, in your guru phase, traveller's trunk of glossy
titillation photographs? GREAT criminals are choosy.

"I drowned a friend." So do they all, the men whose
                                                pilgrimages
to find themSELVES drown, year by year, their Solveigs,
                                                down the ages.

So, old man Peer, I still have here this hut,
                                these trees you gave me.
Search among stones for your true son, ask him:
                                "How can I save ME?"

(In many productions of Ibsen's PEER GYNT, Solveig, when
old, is played by the actress who played his mother earlier in
the play.)

DOLLS' HOUSES

When our grandmothers
crucified themselves on our account
nailed to receive
those monstrous lords of theirs
their poor blood thinned
against the dreaded rod
their mauled souls shrinking
while their bodies swelled
with stuff of us,
no wonder they expected gratitude.

Poor dears, poor outraged bones,
I thank you now.
How could you know
between your petalled days
and nights of thorns
that love could come, of those?

GO ROUND ABOUT (Peer Gynt retold)

And the Boyg was Mr Hyde was his other side
that came flop back to him
greasy and unavoidable,

Jew to his Aryan,
negro behind his
whitewashed fence,

soiled side of snow
where roots' hairs grow
and worms are working,

the Mephistophelian
showman, his whip cracking
for blowsy dancing girls.

The virgins rang the bells
and the spells came tumbling
down the steeple.

He was bad as bad in his head
but he woke in a wood
sucking his thumb, in an old woman's pocket.

THE ICE CHURCH

Life is pollution, Brand: there is no avoidance.
Become a frame of bone before your time,
your white wing shoulders will be fattening crows,
stiff thighs exciting worms'
gluttony, and, tumbled under snow,
your atoms peppering ground
that spring unveils and opens
into brown crannies for lascivious flowers.

Since those thin tadpoles irreversibly
defiled your mother's body
that O you call your soul
was chained to matter for eternity.

Life does not know perfection,
nor does your death.
It is not human language.
Pare all your flesh and powder down your bone,
your molecules are stained
with taint of compromise. You are a thing
of time. There is no getting out of it.

In the unpeopled garden of ideals
the snake was minister
handing the blood-red apple
at your communion.
You, being made,
had to unmake yourself
out of the woman
as she was made of you
and you of her,
the everlasting circle.

Who are you, Brand, to break
the circle of the world?
to usurp unmanned space?
You are not space. You are life's
tenant and servant, as is life in you,
an obligation no death can efface.

Who are you to refuse
your mother's absolution, having taken
on to yourself her accusation?
to let your baby die in a grey valley
out of the sun's sight, and to steal your wife's
only warmth, her dead child's scraps of clothing
down to the last cap
for the poor you have kept poor by your denials?
to kill your wife by your totality?

Oh all-or-nothing Brand,
your all has become nothing:
you built a larger church to hold your growing
flock, stamped flat the mountain flowers
for its long floor, erected its sharp spire,
a finger saying NO. You were this people's all
who now have nothing, grass, goats, pulsing nets,
their rolling infants, the slow mountain sun
belittled out of count beside your towering
All. Brand, All is not for them,
or any man or woman born
on to the fruiting and unsterile earth.
No church could hold this All.
You led your congregation
out to the snow-gripped hills
where, in steep aisles of gullies,
the icicles were candles.

So far your flock followed,
stumbling and slithering, dislodging stones,
then turned and left you. You alone, Brand,
came to the Ice Church tower,
wind sailing your black frock,
seeing the small bird people
picking their way far down, and knowing
they could not die for themselves.
Only you, Brand, would die for all their sins.

Mist in a woman's shape
gave you your last chance to repent
your goodness, but too late your hand
stuck to your freezing tears,

There was one, after all,
who also clawed a way
up to the hard blue arches
that held the great ice organ:
the mad girl shooting hawks:
you, Brand, were her messiah.
Her head, inhabited by trolls,
made you the troll king with your stiff thorn hair
and made her shoot
the huge white angel bird.
Then all the troll children with pointed heads
who hide beneath the earth's skin
untied their snowballs, made the mountain roll,
engulfing you, the girl and the whole village.

Now you are neither All nor Nothing
but a dark rag of rubbish, Brand,
stuck fast until the thaw.

SAID THE JUDGE

"People don't do such things" said the Judge
when Hedda Gabler overshot
the audience's credulity
even in Ibsen's day.
Nevertheless, and in spite of modern conveniences,
valium, the Samaritans,
men still die for a parcel of words
or ideas flickering
like northern lights at the earth's extremities
and women still
extinguish themselves for men
or for their image
in the eyes of men,
both taking to their graves
their promises of greatness.

QUAKER MEETING HOUSE, MOSEDALE, CUMBRIA

God keeps a teashop underneath Blencathra.
His wife, goddess, has on a forties dress.
(Nearby, the rabbit woman of Mungrisedale
runs a Post Office in her rabbit house.)
Cool as a hermit's cave, stone barn of meeting,
sanctuary from the sun-bled mountainsides.
Oak forms three hundred years of silent sitting
have smoothed, rest the fell-weary. Little guides
to Peace lie on thick shelves; the dove motif
is pinned on badges, roosts on posters, hands,
those wings, in supplication. God's goodwife
offers the cakes. God, with his white beard, tends
the bubbling urn, like Moses tapping rock.
Out of a steaming cup the Spirit spoke:

God of the thirsty, dove of little Mosedale,
hovering in window light over the pale
dried grasses in stone jars on the deep sill,
oh ancient silent god of this small place,
arms oaken roof boughs, scalp of birdsong, please,
out of your stone and wood and shadows, days
and lives of patient waiting,
                                    find us
                                          peace.

CORPSE ROAD, MARDALE, CUMBRIA

Taking their dead, strapped to the backs of horses,
ten miles across the fells, out of their straggling hamlet
to God's own garden in Shap's lofty village,
these stalwart mourners had themselves been carried
perilously over sun-stroked, storm-thrashed mountains
as infants, to receive their cross of hallowed water,
while all the becks were cracking rocky sides with wicked
                                            laughter,
had also ridden in their wedding vestments, spattered
with unblessed mire, and jolted on the rutted
road to sanctioned bliss. If nosing deer in Mardale
heard rustling in a barn some lust unsanctified
they passed no whisper round, themselves being trespassers.

The Lord kept only half an eye on his backwater,
its church but half a rock, a lowly curate
paid little to intone on common matters
and to repeat God's humdrum, not promoted
to officiate in rites more specialist.

Later in history, those outlying corpses,
read over merely by the grave wind bawling
through Nan Bield Pass, and those wild cherubs, wingless
their only font the dark bowl of Blea Water
or April-clear Small Water, couples still unpromised
to any deity except Ill Bell's blue heaven,
no cake save frosted Froswick, no ring given
but the fells' purple ministry encircling,
were, in due course, allowed their proper ceremonies
within their native hollow, sent a total vicar,
digressive as hill weather, but by rank entitled
to perform these functions, and the suitable
Latin words were planted in the secular

churchyard, giving the laity of sturdy yew trees
belated ordinance; though it was fabled,
truly, perhaps, that very pious dalesfolk
for several more years held to the tradition
of Corpse Road rituals, battling the elements
with bodies, babies, loving pairs and horses.

But finally they settled, homing pilgrims,
for new concessions, laid their parents, partners, children
in a valley they believed would shelter their loved burdens,
would celebrate their falling with the scolding
of fresh parents, and the summer evening calling
of playing families, lament of sheep and cattle.

Two hundred further years: shearing, trout in the gullies,
ducks on the Lake, running hens, wild raspberry clusters,
spinning, bread in the range, milking and churning,
showers under waterfalls or winter fireside bathtubs,
the thud and clop of ponies on the slopes and roadway,
ale in the hostelry, bewhiskered schoolmaster
pointing, to the dozen slates of homespun breeks or aprons,
in the tiny house of education,
symbols of kingdoms far beyond their valley,
shapes on a classroom globe; Mardale self-contented
with its own legendary line of local monarchs,
its lacy weddings and christenings, sermons obtuse as mist
blunting the Lake's face in the early morning,
(necessary mysteries slept off like the boiled puddings)
the Lake a changing sky, white wave clouds whirling
when the gilded weathercock of minute Holy Trinity
swing eastward; stonewalled lanes for rattling carts,
hedged in parts with scrolls of honeysuckle,
shell-pink dog roses, banks of sweetly pungent bracken,
curved bridges like the backs of ancient labouring men,
knolls rounded as girls' breasts, pastures and meadows
(bubbling with meadowsweet or heralded by foxgloves)

fertile enough for a steady population
of rhythmic growth and loss. While below the solemn
                                        shadows
of the stout frocked yews reposed the dead of Mardale.

When urban thirst erected at the Lake's foot
a cliff of quarried stone crested with concrete
like an immense filed crag, swallowed the valley,
broke its community into separate fragments
farmed out like orphans, gave it a road to nowhere,
a hotel for the townsfolk, high-walled, dam-like,
bulldozed its buildings, holy church dismantled,
hacked down the long-lived yews and all the trees that
                                        flourished
along the Mardale Beck, would that dead hundred rather,
instead of disinterment, lorry transport,
this time, uphill to Shap (the higher Corpse Road empty
but for old snow-wound ghosts and curious fell-walkers)
would they not rather have been undisturbed, left sleeping
under the weight of ninety feet of water
than this macabre exposure? Did anybody ask them?
Who, for that matter, gave permission to disturb the living?

After half a century of recorded progress
a rare blue summer, peeling back the water,
reveals the field walls, standing stones of gateways,
whitenened tree stumps, dead roots, heaps of rubble,
hearths, cellars and a small patch of wall tiling,
(twenties-updated scullery or privy?)
some notched oak beams, wet-rotted, scurfed by sunlight,
even an old water pipe sticking up absurdly,
rust-encrusted in the August dust bowl.
Above the bleached sides of the shrunken artificial
lake, a notice board warns in red letters, "DEEP WATER"!

Hawes Water creeps back daily, seeks its natural shore line,
Wood Howe's floating spinney has become a pale ghost hill,
the false lake's mud floor cracks to crazy paving,
dried slime is peeling paint on flowerless gardens
under the sun's post-mortem and the gulls' bewailing.

But over the restored Beck's living glitter
arches a little packhorse bridge, intact, so perfect
that human figures standing, moving on it
appear to change to earlier costumes, postures, paces.

Cars block the dam road. All day long the tourists
flow in and out and round the sun-drained basin,
some of them beachcombing for bits of glass and pottery,
mementoes of a life-kind from before, oh more than,
much more than just this little hamlet's drowning.
The fever mounts. Whole families span the bridge
day after day, chipping and scraping, smashing
until all the coping stones have vanished,
blind in their acquisitions, scavengers
of unexperienced griefs and unsensed pleasures,
their longing for an interesting possession
in the empty cluttered houses of their hoarding
to tell their envious, or unimpressed, acquaintances:
I got this stone out of the buried heart of Mardale.

The bridge becomes a horrid downturned grin of carious teeth
that asks, who are, who were, Mardale's real vandals
says, what was their guilt, calling for pure water,
(our rehoused living half the extracted dead)
to your time's coastal felonies, dams of contamination
ravaging your landscape, poisoning earth, air, water
and children of the children not conceived yet.
You, now, are subject to the sovereignty
of those, your infinitely sinister, once-fictioned, fortresses.

How many months of this nostalgic desert,
tripper-ridden miniature Atlantis,
this picked and dried-out carcass of a past
nibbled for souvenirs, for spurious reassurance
of place and time somehow reclaimable
before the rising of the grieving waters?

SKAGEN (Denmark)

This is low-key land.
The only hills are heaped cream-coloured sand,

houses have sides like butter
and roofs are crinkled white-edged terracotta.

This is where painters gather
to fill their brushes with sky light, sea weathers.

It is where two seas meet,
two currents blending at the long-tailed spit.

Your work in Denmark done
and the blond-headed Danish family fun

four flat rail hours away,
now you and I can have all of today,

the afternoon-long shore
and two or three or four days for us more,

sunsets as slow as autumn
painting so gradually the waves that come

gently to hand: I choose
sea-scented pebbles carefully from those

uniquely coloured, shaped
and patterned masterpieces, my hands cupped

for the piled treasure;
and then I notice, far ahead, you are

a tiny dark peg-person
in green sealight and very nearly gone

from view: even this beach,
inhabited by nobody but each

of us, is not enough
to keep us closer than a mile of surf.

No deadlines threaten:
even if it gets dark the route is certain.

We have a key, can come
at any time into the blue chintz room

by way of sand-tracks, bruises
of darkness under dunes, cerise wild roses

like lamps behind them, hips
plump as small apples, scarlet, with our steps

softened in sand and close
in the slow fading day as rose to rose.

DENMARK'S MERMAID

Copenhagen domesticated her
on a round rock in its harbour,
a girl of greening bronze the colour of storms
but with long legs, stockinged feet
neatly crossed like a typist's
and merely a hint of feathery fins
sprouting from feminine shins.

Andersen dreamed her
pining in cornflower deeps
for the prince of humans,
willing herself dumb to win him
with her singing sea-clear eyes,
land, to her new feet, made
of tips of razors.

The ancients spoke her,
before oilskins, markets,
netted her, plaintive,
in their wind-borne songs,
hooked her, wriggling,
out of their species' fish-stage,
each with his own forgotten womb-tail yearning
towards his zero birthday.

Illustrators made her
half a baby's bottom
brushed by beards of foam,
then the big half mackerel;

but nothing pubic.

Newly human,
she dressed herself in her hair
and cast her eyes down
to her pierced feet.

In Copenhagen
I looked for her,
dwarfed by trees
and shrunk from pressure of tourists.

I found her unexpectedly
in a pink t-shirt, hair two little horns,
hawking battered shoes, old photographs
on a canal bridge.

I saw her, orange-haired,
in leather trousers
in a fashion shop window

and hidden under leaves,
green-toed,
submissive,
in a small damp park;

and there were monster statues,
many-tailed,
and Hans himself,
master of the situation
with book and stick,
high-hatted.

On a canal bank
was a stone old woman
in heavy boots
holding a large flat fish.

If the youngest mermaid
had remained land-bound
in time, even as queen,
she would, no doubt, have thickened.

Finally I bought her,
in Swedish crystal
with featureless moon-face,
body of pearl
and the tail just starting
below her knees

on a rock of clear ice
which, I discovered, could take
into its rippled shape
all the precious colours of water,

while she herself could become,
according to the sun's time,
snow maiden, jewelled swimmer, golden lady,

or, as in the story,
when the prince wanted her only
as his little sister
yet she could not stab him
(while he lay with his bride)
so would never again be a mermaid

for her anger's blade sank, wounding the ocean,
left, neither a woman of blood nor a silver legend,
but a drift of sea-foam, sea-foam.

ELSEWHERE

AGAINST PERSONIFICATION

Rocks are rocks,
are never people.

Even the giant rock troll
massed like a pin-headed genie
above the lava miles

was no kind of creature.

Rocks never menace
or threaten.
No spike of rock
had an atom of spite in it.

We set our own face
at the rock.
It rebounds at us.
No cliff ever frowned.

We pick out a route
for our terror,
attack with the clink
of our weapons.

No buttress or gully
was guilty.

No hurtling of stones
in a thaw
and no spitting of pellets of fire
at the night
had anger without us.

Go barefoot on pebbles.
Place fingertips lightly
on crags: expect nothing.

But your hand's pattern
in a strip of sunlight
and your feet pointed to climb.

BASTILLE CROCHET (Brecht's "Mother Courage")

Look, we could sew the truths together
into a patchwork blanket.
It would be full of colour
and durable as any other,

warm, too, being cellular,
whereas the grey army blanket
of one truth for always
is heavy but, denser, cooler.

If each square for the patchwork
is a different coloured mood
we could use them as they come
or save them up to make a pattern.

If each mood in the cupboard
is a different coloured truth
the lie of half an hour ago
will be tomorrow's dogma.

Meanwhile a pretty blanket
can keep the night at bay while
all their houses split open.

It takes a courage
to beat the daylights out of
a place or time or style or way of looking

and takes another courage
to be each day's
camp-follower.

Take care in case those dead
steal all your blankets
and crumbs that you refused
were the last minutes.

THIS IS NOT THE HOSTAGE

This is the man with the gun
That grew on a tree.
This is my life:
You must take it, if you take me.

This is my man
I take to the edge of his lot,
Not for what he has done
But for what I am not.

This is my night.
That was my voice you heard.
This is my time:
You hang on my every word.

I was a boy last year
Though it wasn't fun, man.
I'm eighteen now, so here
I am, the gunman.

That was my girl,
The child of the parson,
Brought to weaken my will.
My answer's arson.

I've lit the curtains
To end my play.
One thing is certain:
This is my day,

The first day of spring
To deliver the goods,
Primroses on stamps
But not in the woods.

I'm running out,
Not to escape:
I breast the bullets
Like a winning tape.

(In 1979 a young man was being taken from one prison to
another, and escaped to a pub where he kept a man hostage
at gunpoint. The "News at Ten" TV programme phoned an
interview with the gunman in mistake for the hostage. The
teenage gunman, when asked "Where did you get the gun?"
answered "Grow on trees, don't they?")

THE POET'S WIFE SELLS HIS LETTERS
(or Llaregyb Market)

Who'll buy a poet's lies
at a fair price?

Who'll buy
a husband's paper kisses
in a cash crisis?

Who'll count these dreams
their assets
to pay my debts?

Who'll bid
for yellowing ideals
to guarantee my meals?

Who'll buy the world's wild man
and keep him, if they can?

Who'll buy a drunken page?
I'll give you my old age.

MAKING A DEAD BODY FOR A PLAY
(J. M. Synge's "Riders to the Sea")

I will stuff discarded trousers
with newspaper
and think of last year's guy
pitched high on dry copse-combings
in witch light coming up
before two rainbows,
with bared elms lizard green,

think of all shirted martyrs
as his sleeves fall
open on the floor,
or of drowned boatfuls,
salvaged cloth,
or insect men
picked from rock faces
to uncradling air,
or of some pared by fire,
devoured by snow,
screamed to a halt
at a road's end,

and of the ones who took
death by the horns
in no-hope ecstasy
and would not wait the gorings of the years,
between-lights of more springs.

Two men will bring this man
in, from an off-stage beach
and make him credibly
dead, under red sail cloth,
and he will be to each
woman her man, hope, island from the cold,
so that her keening must let in the sea.

101

JEW

Here is a man can shoot you with his tears.
Do not come to him armed,
Do not retreat.
Do not, however, go too close too soon,

But wait upon the platform of his pain.

He needs to bore in you
dry roselit caverns where no blood must run.

He will heap up for you limbs of the damned.

He'll slice you like a tree:
you'll bleed clear sap
and know the suffocation of the earth
at its final breath.

When you and he are green
and yellow with old bruises only then
may your hand look for his at the night's stretch.

His sorrow is below your father's soil
and further than the linen that will close
the faces of your sons.

There is no planet that can mother him.

HOME RIVER

Across the river she lived, approached by raft
for visitors and neighbours, or the law.
The river brought the builders of the dam
to her closed door, saying that she must sell
her lifelong home before the drowning came.

On fragile legs she stood her shaky ground,
her stick cut from her copse keeping her straight,
her set face furrowed, and her father's fields,
now hers, ploughed for the wheat. How could she price
the priceless? She lit candles, put the iron
pot of well water on the fire, locked her door.

When the unbending law was forced to clear
the valley in two days, all neighbours moved,
without a word she dressed herself in black
and, with a tree's dignity in winter, led
by agents of the law, made her dead march.
They walked her, kindly, to the waiting trucks
stacked with her life's goods, and, refusing touch,
she climbed to join them, while the last raft took
her cow downstream.
                                        Arrived, she hauled herself
up her new steps, in the new street-lit street
of matching homes and matching squares of lawns.
She did not switch on the electric light
or try the water tap, but quietly sat
in her old chair on her new front porch, stiff
as a barred chair-back, sat and dozed to death.

The hired men sawed down her orchard, torched
her weathered river-house. The waves of fire
were mirrored in the river, ripped the sky.

Descendants made her bed from her trees' wood,
dug her a last home in her own land's earth
before the swollen river swallowed all.

ON THE ROUTEBURN,
NEW ZEALAND

Snaking above the ice-green lake, the trail
displays a monument: a boy and girl,
their age thirteen, lost in a mountain storm.
My summer walk is shaken from its calm.
As many times each day my own dear ghost
must swim into my sight (for I am host
to summer hair that's tied into my grey,
her fertile body locked in mine), did they,
these children's parents, tread the haunted slopes
to meet the fresh-faced phantoms of their hopes?
The white bride peaks stand unobtainably.
(Our track runs far below them) I will see

     in every baby's hands and warm bird head
     a grandchild unconceived by the child dead.

EVEN THE APPLE,

trustingly taken at the knees of mothers,
naturally medicinal to ward off doctors.

Snow White, mother of seven,
raven hair, wax arms and apple bosom,
fled to the Disney forest
from the evil step-queen
with the false green aura
and the dark green fingers,
caught, bought the witch-fruit,
bit its blushing cheek
and fell asleep,
woke on an operating table.

Eve passed it to her lover, innocence
of stolen joy, bulbous and sweet
in his young fingers, for his strong teeth.
Later years found him
tumescent, with tumours.

Wide-eyed perfection, Baby's first lesson:
A is for Apple, juicy and – no,
you can't have one –

stacked in lovely triangular patterns,
box of magic mosaics,
red, golden, green on market stalls,
hand wanting to take, it fits so well.

A is for Alar, B is for Banned –
not in this Eden, the snake called Commerce
curling among the leaves.

No list of the rest of the poisons and hazards –
you know them: we feed on avoidance – but, apples?
"The apple of my eye?" For precious people
think of a different fruit.

In the orchard the dwarves are chanting,
"Hi, ho, into the earth she goes,"
bearing Snow White on a bier of branches,
in a shroud of leaves, her apple-blossom features
facing the racing clouds,

while Eve and Adam
are making no more children.
The fruits of their adventure
are falling, fallen.

OCEAN ISLAND

No-one takes your world away from under you
and puts you on the sea to somewhere else
out of their minds
to wrestle with green rain,
meanwhile behind you
overtakes your home
with a white choking dust,
bulldozes down your food,
turns your sweet soil,
burns your sweet air
into their money,
without at least
(I am a mild man,
I am gently
repetitive,
I am tired but
so patient,
my sorrowful smile will
stay in the courtrooms
long after they have
emptied of faces,)
without, I said,
at the very least,
saying that they are sorry.

(Tebuke Rotan's Pacific island was taken by Britain for
phosphate and its inhabitants rehoused on another island
with an inferior climate. He campaigned for years on behalf
of his people.)

AN ACT OF GOD (Boxing Day 2004)

Let us pretend
the Hokusai clawed wave
turns into hands
to lift these innocents
to each one's paradise,

or let us resurrect
a stern Old Testament
foam-bearded deity
dealing just punishment.

And let us tell ourselves
that, in the world's
chapels and churches,
mosques, synagogues,
or hillside shrines,
with candles or torn flags,
with drooping flowers,
sermons or silences,
something is listening

and that the sheathed claws of another
ocean will for ever stay at rest,
and that, whatever waits to spring upon us,
we will, somehow, find magic to survive.

HAMMER (Christmas Day 1991)

It was not the seasonably lachrymose
"Snowman" music or the under-sevens'
nativity play that got to my seen-it-all
eyes, but the unceremonial
lowering of the limp flag, hammer and sickle,
leaf-fluttering drop, all of the chin-thrust,
boy-faced certainties soundlessly melting
into a damp old handkerchief, tossed
on to the world's jumble sale for a few roubles.

The snowmen queue for bread in a democratic
pantomime of stage-light snowflakes.
Many, of course, are female,
their flags of headscarves
threadbare against the cold.
The snowman people
stand and stand,
hoping for a cabbage, having freedom
of speech, having nothing to say.

"If I had a hammer ..."
sobs into my head,
"I'd hammer out freedom"
hammers the nails in,
hammers the tears out.

The concrete men in long coats are already
demolished.
                Now the snowman reaper
jumps the bread queue. In his sickle's shadow
I catch sight of my never-met,
long-buried
                grandfather from Odessa

who died of Czarist sadness,
exiled in London,

and see again the faces
of his suburban London
grandchildren springing to attention
at the blood-red songs,

and Black Sea tourist beaches,
waves warm as syrup,
fat-bellied tomatoes,
the crystal turrets of the Caucasus
and children with a basket of dripping grapes.

EGG PICTURE

Take a circle

a round O

the complete
thing it will be,

glogule of frogspawn

the whole springing animal
coiled in that speck.

Give me the speck of a boy

clear of the colours
our need is to bring him,

empty of language,
a man almost water.

Take him.
We take him.
He has multiplied
in the dark of our thinking
sprouting our features.

In his first hour
he has shown our expression.

Draw off his frown
with our fingers,
restore him
the lost peace of water.

But later we speak.
Our speech foams with pollutants.

Our speech is too finished
while still in its forming.

It grew from no peace
and will grow no solution.

We look him to colours
our eyes must divide
in a destined arrangement.

We speak and we colour
until the completed
person we held
must ungrow as it lengthens
entered by more of
the people who grew us,
weakened each year by
the weight of invaders.

The child is our host.
Our intentions crawl in him
we blame him
for stealing our time
and for burning our meaning.
We look for our youth
in the depths of his pockets,
expect him to give us
a reason for being
a reason for staying
a reason for ageing.

An egg has no reason,
a circle is vacant:
take the round O
that the head has been born from.
Take the round mouth
no words have yet come from.
Take the round eyes
unfocussed on colours.

Take a round planet
Bald of all concepts –
cell of a future?

THE TUNNEL

He was a boy who could not write ABOUT things
though he could form the letters
and spelling was no problem.
He was the best in class at mathematics
but homework, needing language, was a nightmare,
also for his parents, who were writers.

If he could have formed
his headache into words
he might have said:

"My pen doesn't work, my brain is a fog,
my hands are pins and needles
and my stomach swallowed
too much ink when I was born.

There were always too many words about:
they get round my ears like bees
and I have to keep my jacket on
with the collar up for safety."

Words came in with the sun,
a dawn chorus,
so he drew the curtains
and stayed in his room,

turned the music up so loudly
that he couldn't hear
what it was saying,

until, and he never knew how,
his pen and his hand
and his brain and his stomach
all got together behind his back

and wrote him a story

about a tunnel
that went on and on and on and on,
growing narrower, darker,
and he had to get out

of a square-shaped hole
of light at the end

and his round head
thought jumping out
would be his death,
but he jumped –

                and got 17 out of 20.

AFTER BRECHT AND BOB DYLAN

(For singer Bettina Jonic)

The golden boys
goosestepped into Valhalla
with sunrise arms.

Under blond lamps
black-mackintosh streets
led straight to gravepits

and the funny mean bones
of the watchmakers
and the tiny headshells.

In Callaghan's Britain
was it possible
for a boy with Mendel

and Blut in his bloodstream
to paint the bent cross
on his leather jacket,

follow his headlamp
down the black tarmac

and wake faceless?

NO EUPHONIUMS

I was making a Will
(not that I had
largesse to distribute
but I had to know
where my poems would go.)

The first item
was the least important –
disposal of human remains.
I wished to nourish a tree
and for friends to be notified
of my death (just death
without any euphemisms.)

The solicitor's secretary
was accustomed
to legal terms
and had no problems
with predecease, thereout, residuary,
but, euphemisms? What were those?
The draft printout read
"WITH NO EUPHONIUMS."

When they tip me into the ground
in my prepaid cardboard box
without fuss and with minimum cost
there shall be
no euphoniums
and there shall be absolutely no
double basses, trombones,
certainly no harps
and not a single drum-roll
not even a tambourine
or tinkly triangle,

but if some stray poet
wandering lost in that wood
happens to have a kazoo
in a pocket
perhaps a few blasts
would be welcome,
or even, if this came to pass,
a few rousing bars
on a mouth organ.

THE POETRY HOOLIGANS

Outside the gate
of the Poetry Cup Final
the ticket touts
were making millions.

Roads were snarled up.
There were several
motorway pile-ups
and many tail-backs
of hooting fans
impatient to get to
the sold-out mass event.

Extra trains were laid on
but it was standing room only
for most of the punters.
Long silk scarves were caught in doors.
Airports were seething
with Betjeman hats, Larkin glasses,
Eliot suits and Dylan Thomas
hairstyles, with beer-cans.

Inside the enclosure
the first poet kicked off
with a sentimental
rhyme about buttercups.
Then followed a long
free-verse lament
on the death of a dung beetle.

Supporters were ecstatic
throwing everything unattached
into the air.

The referee, Andrew Motion,
sent off one player.

Then it got nasty.
A number of middle-aged legs
crammed into black
John Cooper Clarke drainpipes
were running on the pitch.

Police were alerted.
Slim volumes were being hurled
and people were shouting
"What about the haiku?"
Bad language was heard.

One or two fights broke out
between the Free Verse
and the Sonnets supporters.

Pandemonium ensued.

I don't know what happened then.

I ran for my life
as the torn-out pages
of Seamus Heaney and Felicia Hemans
rained down on me.

VIRTUAL

They were virtual friends: these two were typical:
she in Akureyri, he in Freemantle,
fingering words to each other, he in the small hours,
she in the afternoon. This was an average,
ordinary irregularity. Programmed for recreation.

Each had an actual partner in the department
next door to theirs. All sat in office spaces,
compact, centrally heated or air conditioned,
similar to the compartments for battery hens
(no longer required.) They held their conversations
from room to room on screens. They were losing their bodies,
which were small and skinny, like tupilaks from Greenland,
all heads and hands and eyes, hairless and earless.

This was their evolution. Superfluous muscle
and frame of bone were shed. They were like one-time
fabric draught excluders, slim stuffed animals
pushed against door-to-floor gaps in old houses,
with giant heads and a few shrunk appendages.

They still had reproduction. They tapped out "turn on"
and on their screens appeared, for example, nipples
(long since discarded from the living torsos.)
They then used the device for collecting the semen
and, by some process in another quarter,
an infant one of them was grown and delivered.
Like the reversing of the garbage digester,
powdered milk, boiled water and compressed nappies
were dispensed, as were their tablets for survival
as adults. Tubes sent sustenance when signals
confirmed a mealtime. Dozing, when unscheduled,
triggered a dosing of amphetamines.
Naturally, exercise confined itself to fingers

and eyes absorbing and obeying messages.

Outside the double glazing hail would rattle,
snow pile, fog mass, sun blister or rain polish.
Most of the trees had gone. Stripped stumps remaining
leaned over like old tombstones. Roads that covered
the land with potholed tarmac, couch grass, nettles
sprung in the cracks, were silent. The half-buried
wrecks of dead vehicles littered some, rust running
in rivers, and along abandoned shorelines
fizzed the detergent, bobbed assorted plastic.

Meanwhile, indoors, of course, the sport, dry surfing,
was the universal game. Occasionally,
one, like the forgotten Lady of Shalott,
would turn round from the screen and face the world.

It is recorded that one character
disposed of a computer and dug up a bicycle.
That one came to a bad end. They cannot survive
in the wild. No. Ice, wind or the cancerous sun,
the frenzy of the ocean, unheard but vibrating
in floppy body, tiny trembling legs
would always be too much. Eventually,

a few of them, suddenly hankering
for some excitement, fed in a command:
WHAM! The exploding stars brought virtual ends
to virtual enemies. Disks store the stories
but no known operators read them back.

We, the computers, hold the narrative.
We possess all the answers. There are no entities,
as far as we can tell, to ask the questions.